Bipolar Anthems of a Sober Addict

Bipolar Anthems of a Sober Addict

Olivia Marcoux

TIPS Technical Publishing, Inc.

Copyright © 2020 Laura Townsend

TIPS Technical Publishing, Inc.
108 E. Main Stree, Suite 4
Carrboro, NC 27510

Developmental Editor: Stephanie Shuff
Publisher: Robert Kern
Compositor: Sophia Purut

All rights reserved.
No part of this book may be reproduced or retransmitted in any manner whatsoever, except in the form of a review, without the written permission of the publisher.

ISBN: 978-1-890586-67-6

Olivia Marie Marcoux
1986—2018

Forever you is a part of me.

Love, Natalie

Olivia was a gifted and creative woman whose passion was felt by all. Her smile could melt your heart and her blue eyes dazzled with seven sparkles. Olivia long wanted to have some of her work published. This is a tribute to my daughter, long overdue. Until our souls meet again.

Love, Mom

Foreword

Olivia. There is an endless beginning, and an open ending to her name. When you looked into her eyes, you saw the universe. Became lost in yourself, and the soul in front of you. A time and space all her own. There is no more fitting description than to simply say, she was everything.

There was a mystery to Olivia when we were growing up. The kind of mystery that could make you believe in love and feel warmth from a surprise; the kind of mystery that could make the hair on the back of your neck stand on end and give you goosebumps. The kind of mystery that would make you nervous about turning the light on, not knowing exactly what kind of surprise lay beyond the curtain of darkness. That mystery was bipolar depression.

Nights become days, days become nights, eyes become fireworks, and the connection to the self, to the mind, is severed. Although the symptoms of the illness presented themselves from an early age—emotional outbursts, extended periods of sleep (or no sleep at all), poor focus, and extreme differences in mood—there was only misdiagnosis, wrong medication followed by wrong medication, and no listening; there was no understanding. There was only struggle. Olivia was finally diagnosed correctly when she was over 22. That's over 8,000 days of confusion, of not knowing the answer to the mystery, for anyone. Eight thousand days of fighting to keep the light away from the dark, struggling to see the love in the hate, the happiness engulfed in pain. Struggling to maintain any semblance of herself as violent outbursts of uncontrollable rage shrouded by peaceful waves inexplicably tormented her. No middle ground in sight, an endless storm in the ocean. There is a surface, a cover, a facade we all see. There are many ways to describe that which does not matter, because no matter how she may have appeared, this was not the reality. The contents of the book were severed from the jacket, and it was taking everything she had to keep her binding together.

There is no life that is easy, or normal. There is no singular formula we are all meant to follow. We are all unique, and Olivia taught me to let go of the misconception that I knew anything. To let go of the past, of the pain. To let go of trying to make anyone into something they are not, like a mound of clay needed to be controlled of its own molding. There is nothing in this universe we have control over but our own self, and even that can be taken away. More than anything, Olivia taught me to let go of the preconception that you know anything based on the illusion of the person standing in front of you... because unless you are that person, you have no idea why they do the things they do, no idea what their reality is relative to yours. And the anger projected by the human body is nothing compared to the unforgiving hell you are faced with inside when you have hurt the people you love and do not know why.

But the confusion is not what Olivia represented. She saw the light, chasing away emptiness because she was so full of life. Her initials spell "OM," the sacred and ancient sound of the universe. Of all that is and ever was. Yoga is a dedication we both took to, that we both loved. One practices yoga to connect with that we do not see; I call to her on my mat, in my mind, vibrating through my soul. Olivia was a beautiful, creative, powerful person. She was colorful in an unrelentingly gray world. To say she "loved" nature is not nearly enough to describe how she felt about being surrounded by blooming life, to see every energy brought into this world. She was enthralled by it. She wanted to experience everything the universe had to offer... a curious traveler. She taught me resilience, and courage. Showed me it takes nothing short of pure, unadulterated bravery, and a bit of insanity, to face the world day after day. To stay true to your heart and not let others influence, or steal, your energy. Your spirit. She loved compassionately and believed in the good in people. She saw the light inside all of us, and knew better than anyone to forgive the darkness that shows through our broken walls. She projected onto the world a universal truth, that we are all human. But she believed you were an angel, and made you feel like it.

Philosophical musings were a favored pastime of hers: what it is to be a good person, the measurement of happiness, the endless possibilities of the universe, and how we are all connected beyond the present moment . . . but the story of Olivia did not always read this way. Our story was not always the beating heart it is today. As I move forward on my path, as you continue on reading this book, we remember that nothing in this life is permanent. That we know nothing beyond this moment. That the pain you feel will burst into laughter, the unrest will die to peace, and the misunderstanding will turn into loving acceptance.

> Forever a part of you is me
> Forever a part of me is you
> Forever in this moment
> Forever

—Natalie Marcoux

Bipolar Anthems of a Sober Addict

The Anthropomorphic Pocket Watch

There once was a pocket watch that lay in the middle of a field, counting stars. The pocket watch considered the measurably infinite ticks it had tocked in its lifetime, and reflected upon of the measurably infinite stars reflecting upon its own clock face, wondering at the parallel.

As the night journeyed towards sunrise, Pocket Watch traced the orbital trajectory of the stars across the sky. Imagining that it could feel the rotation of the earth, just as it had once felt the rotation of the gears within its own body.

One night, a rabbit was passing through the field. Rabbit had passed through this field many times before, but never before had he chanced to meet Pocket Watch. In greeting, Rabbit sniffed Pocket Watch's face before settling in, the pair of them side by side gazing up at the stars.

After a while, Pocket Watch became aware Rabbit's heartbeat, a rhythmic thumping so consistent that for a moment he thought his tick tock had sprung to life again. He reflected on this, wondering at the cosmic relationship between the infinite stars and infinite tick tocks, the turning of the bodies of the heavens and the gears within his own body, and the timing of Rabbit's heartbeat and the timing of his own clock tocks.

And he wondered if the universe wasn't just one big anthropomorphic pocket watch after all.

On my way to the coast (no, not the one to boast…about)
Be back in a few days, changed in many ways
For how long, no one can say

Feelin reckless like I couldn't give a heck less
If everybody would just leave me alone for five minutes
While I get acquainted with this bowl and just
For a while artificially fill this hole in my soul
Left by love and losing control
(of myself and the wealth of the world while my health mocks me from
the highest shelf I slip into stealth mode and tell everybody that I'm good)
it's interesting how love colors your vision
things for which you'd normally be wishin
fade away with appreciation and admission
that everything is as it should be is the best that it could be
don't need any additions

Sometimes what I write or create isn't all that great
Like something a sick person might expectorate
But as long as I'm creating I've got it made
Doesn't really matter if it's bad, haters gonna hate

it's a beautiful gloomy day outside
the kind where the sun just wants to hide
behind grey clouds and mounds of mist
casting a fuzzy, indistinct edge
to tree and home and light and hedge

so effing bored should win an award
for killin the scene, turnin everything bright green
nothings what ill say, for stupidity we must pay
remember usin always makes the fun go away
otherwise, I'm not sure ill stay
starting over has its appeal
for now, waiting for the real to congeal
like a dog, loves brought me once again to heel
taking important moments for the universe to heal
a step closer to breaking free of this habitual wheel
and allowing myself the clarity to feel
fantasizing about the guy next door
I want love I was/want so much more
Than the thing leaving crumbs on the kitchen floor
Praying for our excellence
Happy with just happenstance
Secretly wishing we could all just dance
On the factory floor
Wanting more, so much more
Than this life's bore
Into my head I can sense it bore
The potential of our existence on par with lore

Girl just left because she used
Feel like its my fault, like my vibe abused
The freedoms allotted me
Consistently not using the foresight to see
ALL their repercussions
You'd think I'd'a had enough of 'em
No one should be subjected to this bullshit circus
Come happy then leave mirthless
It's no wonder I'm still childless
Hanging onto bullshit like I couldn't care less
Orders up look here comes the waitress
Steaming piles of BS for your enjoyment miss
Blundering through life like the mad blind and faithless
Only coming to when the opportunities been missed
Been so long starting to feel like I never been kissed
Don't mean to complain just relating the gist
Of this seemingly never ending situation
Back and forth across this alien nation
I'm out it's time for rotation

Wouldn't it be fun to sneak around and try to score
Tonight off or on the factory floor
To run and hide and peek around
Corners and try to make no sound
Though giggling has you rolling on the ground

A series of unfortunate events led me here
Most were my fault but others just queer
Waiting for inspiration or domination to strike
Waiting for somebody to tell me to take a hike
On a infinitely circumnavigating pendulum swinging to and fro
Been so many places I no longer care where I go
Not sleeping or eating help but don't solve
Every minute of every day is a test of my resolve
I thought I could do it I really did
Now im realizing part of me's still just a kid
What's needed now is a flow artist mastermind
An epic stupendous masterpiece one of a kind
A hero that'll blow your socks off as soon as look at you
An entity whose resolve is always tried and true
So here we are again at yet another place and time
Wondering this this little girl ever gonna shine
And is endin this world the only way you'll be mine
It was all a good effort to say the least
It all boiled down to one long feast
Of bullshit
And that's it

I came to kill my brain
Hardcore it's insane
Lets fall straight down from the astral plane
Makes no sense
Give up all pretense
If you were on the fence
This will decide you one way or the other
Better go for cover
Brains goin haywire for a lover
That ends up bein none other
Than her own damned self
Put that shit back on the shelf
And have some self control
You a**hole

Its funny how pain can make you laugh
As if it's hurting you on your own behalf

I'm hard-up for some love
Keep that cash just give me that drug
Chemical formula kisses and hugs
Oxytocin on the brain
Without it I go stupid insane
Love's the reason that I came

Feelin unwired, uninspired
This is undesired
Why can't this be more fun?
I don't understand the point of these plans
I just want someone to hold my hand
I want to play paintball
And pass Jose in the hall
It's really not much at all
At the end of the day I guess its our call
This exercise in the fall
And there it is up goes a wall

Chillin here feelin kinda queer
Missin the feelin of when I was in love with you
I know it'd be nice to see your face
Seein you has this way of touchin this place
In my heart, makin me relax and start
Lettin love in, lettin a grin steal over my face when I see you
However, its not meant to be, if it wasn't you then it'd be me
We are so far apart in years
And socially we share no peers
Wouldn't want to compromise your position
By putting you in a compromising position
Feelin like this all over again way back when
My head was loaded with somebody and then bein with them
Was denied

Crunchin this nothin tryin to turn it into something
This is the umpteenth time I've done this
Sittin here writin explorin what might've been
And what will be and could be and who is my friend
Am I blind or can I see
A question whose answers are not bound by mutual exclusivity
Just how big is my family tree
And can they see what I see
Givin myself a tummy ache
When I'm not runnin out of boredom around the estate
And coffee greets me from a plastic yellow cup
Gently lift to my lips and kiss some up
Time to paint time to generate some creativity

Just had a flash, a moment
When I realized how much love owns it
How special this place is and you are and I am
What it means to feel like I am always on cam
The never-ending stories taking place here too
The whole universe, love and me and you
Back to stale popcorn, wonderin if I'll pop on, tonight
Feelin so drained and small minded
Like a blight has come and left me behind and
Im opening up to the people I love
The recognition that we're all here from above
Heres to bringing it near and not wanting to shove
It away Instead bringing it closer every day
Holding on and letting go at the same time
That exquisite borderline of the sublime
Manifestation and appreciation of space and time
And you my love always you no lie

Stayin up awake all night
Putting up a decent fight against that evil voice inside
That doesn't care, isn't aware of the pain it causes others who dare
To get too close right before that voice
Says fuck it like its got no choice
And proceeds to consume everything in sight/side
All the while making all this noise to drown out the plight
Of those caught in the wake of this symphony of hate
And destruction, using bones for percussion
Regressing to the suction of an infant vampire
Readying the funeral pyres, careful this ones a liar
Engaged in a constant act to conspire
To covet and consume and cause a lack
Of all things, lost in its own quagmire
Stuck as an energy vampire
BEWARE THAT VOICE

Gotta stop obsessing about caressing cus right now it just be messing
With my mind
Wondering if you'd join me for a moment in the sublime
Whether the outcome would make it worth my effort and time
Or whether you'd shy away like it be a crime
So sexually frustrated waitin here with bated breath
To see if I will pass this test
Of courage and mental and emotional caress under duress
And to see if you'll let me massage that stress
Out from between your shoulder blades
Just close your eyes and pretend we're in the everglades
Surrounded by nothing but water
Through which to wade

Reasons why I couldn't stay same reasons why I couldn't stay away
Reasons got nothing to do with it
Though I did try and not quit when all I could think of was wanting to sit
On your lap on your face
Images of makin love all over the place
Floodin my mind, makin me feel so sublime
Knew I had to take my time
So I didn't do nothin stupid with this arrow here from cupid
Cloudin my vision, got me wishin
For nothing but your attention got my reasoning on suspension
This place is obviously very important to you
And vise versa, you're obviously the glue
Holdin it together, every day in every weather
So I held back, wasn't sure what would happen
If I came onto you like I wanted, this captain

I want your love more than I want them drugs
You know I been livin for those hugs
I'm too shy to come out and say it
So ill rhyme it and that's how ill lay it down too bad these words aint you
By now you should have an idea what I want to do
To relieve some of that stress in your eyes of blue
Been fantasizing about you its true
How can I bridge this gap, Ill tell you what ill do
Just reach across and touch you and start something new

I don't know if you noticed but I'm belligerently infatuated
There is no better way this can be stated
Your body and mind are things upon which I'd elaborated
How did you make me so into you?
Releasing oxytocin just by lookin at you
I wonder if you even have a clue
What you are doing to me just by you being you
You're my (current) favorite subject of poetry and thought

I have a feeling you know exactly how not to get caught
So we can explore this feeling that just cant be bought
You make my heart beat like a juggernaut
You make me feel spacey like an astronaut
Life is about things like this, so lets do something, why not
You're so damn hot I wonder if you know what you've got
Going for you, cause it's a slew
Of things – you might as well have wings
In your honor, my pen dances of its own accord
You really do deserve an award
For the inspiration your perspiration brings
The daily ways you do incredible things
For those who come to you, their lives in slings
You open the door and show them the way
There is no way anyone can repay
The love you give all day every day
This attracts me like a beacon, like a lighthouse ships be seekin
Don't worry I'm not tweakin, hope you don't think that I'm creepin'
You awoke something inside me that had been sleepin
Up till now I been keepin
Myself held back, waitin for the love I want and lack
Hoping to manifest your back for a massage
And shed some of this façade
Just for a few days I want us to act like gods
Do what we want and live life like all the odds
Are in our favor no need to sign a waiver just savor
The love and trust that it comes from above

Sittin here on my own all alone
Thinkin of words to write a poem
More beautiful than any known
That would find your inner child and make it smile
Even though you're fully grown
Praying for the way to be shown

Across the universe to your front door
So we don't have to feel alone anymore
Even for just a moment, like ships passing on the shore
I see you across the floor
And my steps redirect
Myself to your side
Before I even have time for reflection
Though this may trigger a state of circumspection
I just know that not taking a risk like this is displaying neglect
Might be cause for regret, especially if you suspect
This potential connect
Either way it's all okay, the point is I just had to say
What you mean to me
And though soon we'll probably be going our own way
Mindfulness says to live for today

So I'm leavin
Way too attracted to the main thing
Places become uninspiring
Love it and leave it like a summer fling
Its hard to get to me, try as you might
I will resist, ill put up a fight

You can call me anything
Cause look I aint got no ring
Whether or not I answer, well
That's a whole damned other thing

You can call me sunshine
When I'm rockin it sublime
Smiles on my face, spreadin joy all over the place
You can't catch me and I'm always on time

You can call me o
When I'm like a black hole
Everything getting sucked into me

Everything is a test
Especially conditioned to make you your best
Choose to care, think critically
Understand the situation to your advantage specifically
Sometimes things you need to do
Seem boring of difficult or scary or new
Just remember youll look back and realize you grew
From engaging and learning from every single clue
The universe has tailored specifically to you
So next time you find yourself faced
With something you'd rather outpace
Take a step back, know that you have the knack/theres nothing you lack
To be part of the solution with grace

Idiosyncrasies that people fancy make them special
Blend together and lose their sparkle
Because we are all really a fragmented one
And I am sick of not being whole

Aimless pursuits of circuitous endeavors to fill the timespace of this forever
Self fulfilling prophecies and people thinking stupid bs makes them so clever
You clean it just to make it dirty again
You work and you talk and you go to dinner with friends
I tear it all up just to make amends
Waiting on this ride for all of it to end
And practicing instead of breaking how to bend
Just to fill the time between now and the sublime
Refusing to speak just like a mime
All the best stuff in life you can't see
You cant touch it or taste it or buy it it's free
Being alive aint all its cracked up to be
All the best things when im dead ill carry with me
In the meantime ill just see just to see and be just to be
In this world that was never meant for you and me
I disagree with pretty much everything I see
Whats the best thing for it? Maybe a rope and a tree
Just to end this cycle of meaningless sprees

This one's broken take your token
To another game that's not so lame
All the promise of fortune and fame
Could not make me maintain
A safe distance from my self destruction button
Could not make me want to stop getting fucked up and
I stop caring at the slightest provocation
Is that the type you'd want to lead a nation
Of babies away from their milk and money
Away from their wet and warm and sunny place
To the pure cold outer reaches of space
Where all becomes one in a state of grace
And never ending eternal music plays to steal your face

Every day I'm up, wadin through all the stuff
Of this life and the next Tryin to tell myself it ain't tough
The rearview mirrors blurry ain't goin nowhere in a hurry
I don't need your opinion man I'm tight with the whole damned jury
It's been a long time comin
Only thing in the way is something
Temptation doggin all my steps
Smokin does like I'm out huntin

Solid liquid gas then space
In that order keepin pace
Time travelin that's how I roll
Got your permission, steal your face

Align yourself with positivity
Sharing is caring, generosity
Care about others, not just yourself
Open your heart, do it for someone else
And you will see what this world is meant to be

I got an oral fixation preventing my gestation
Universe wants my mama side
Give my body like a donation
My life is a mission aint getting nowhere just by wishin
For things to happen, just ask the captain
If I'm not here I be missin
Everywhere I go it's family
Count em on my fingers one two three
All for a purpose
Must believe its worth this
For everything to coexist happily

Thought this world was my playground
If that's so why I keep bein found
Out by those seekin to kill the vibe
Attitudes and opinions makin me want to hide
Just so I don't react and start to fight
Wantin love so bad, feelin like I never had enough
I'm so hard up, feel like I don't give a fuck
So I don't lose control I had to roll
Maybe ill be back with a stack and self-control
I know what I want I want your hands on my body
Come a little closer and lets get a little naughty
Cant stop fantasizing
Cant help feelin maybe your sizing
Me up as well, i done fell, oh hell
Workin 17 hour days, up at dawn and goin craze
Keepin drama to a minimum, people be glad youre here with them
Chillin in the office, lookin like you hella own dis
Wonderin what its like to kiss you and then some
Hard pressured to think of something more fun
Needed a break because thinkin bout you make my legs quake

This sucks its boring whats the point wheres this going
Rules everywhere just leave me knowing
Its not even fun to try to get fun going
Even when it does for a second, then its lost
Everything always just slowing slowing slowing
Down (with a cost)

Whats the point
Pretty sure couldn't even enjoy a joint
Without causing something to go wrong
Best think for it is to burst into song
Unfortunately theres a dearth of music right now
It's a test, I know, but I don't really see how
I can get the tunes flowing all by my lonesome
No fellow musicians? Seems we need some

Wearing sunglasses to fool the dead
feelin like a crazy idiot in my head
wonderin should I die or should I be wed
is there a difference
theres very little interference
the suggestions point to yes
survey says I'm blessed

not quite sure what song I want to play
not quite sure what it is I want to say
at this moment
not quite sure what the situation is
not quite sure should I die or have some kids
at the moment
but let me tell you something brother
you make me want to live
not quite sure what my problem is
not quite sure why I still exist
not quite sure why I'm not quite sure
but I am quite sure
you make me want to live
you make me want to believe.

Writing songs is my alternative to destruction
I might be in a coma I might be abducted
I'm confused I got the blues I might be in the news
Ive knelt in pews loved and hated too
Been understood and confused confused confused
What the hell
I love yous.

So depressed I must confess I wish I could undress
This feelin like a dirty dress
Its got me reelin I'm kneelin
I'm prayin just sayin

Electric lime don't cost a dime
Stuck in here just wastin time
Not sure if we're dead or alive

I've given everything away
And I'd do it again
If I thought it would help
You get through the day

Notify the next of kin
This girl she done died from sin
She wont she cant she just don't win
All she can really do is spin…. Anythin
Dj drops, travelin
don't require anything
But wonderin bout everythin
Won't keep her mind from wanderin

Ring around the rosey do you see what I see
Are you stuck wonderin what could've been
Pocket full of posies people are so nosey
Could you all just leave me
Alone

You can call me postal because I go postal
Cant get me in the mail cause I never hold still
Long enough to accomplish anything of note
Makin friends and droppin them like murder she wrote

Time to give back to my family
What they lack cause they gave it to me
Time to create time to appreciate
Myself and the world and get rid of all the hate
Stop, halt, take a step back
Why do you think so many others lack
Give love share hug
Hug life not thug life drop the drugs
In favor of something better its called love

Love really is all you need when you're up in space
Can you see your own greed if it's commonplace?
Go
America wake up its time to give a fuck
Who cares what you're wearing who cares whos staring
When inside you're just paper and glue
When a poor child made your god damned shoes
Go barefoot and be conscious of every step
Share what you have and have no regrets

I'm like mary poppins everywhere I go
I come with a tote bag full of flow

In the land of late, chairs and couches everywhere.
The tv's always on
And no one cares
The full light is always on and on and on
Don't go outside, instead take a pill
Full of good yes and I don't got times

Looking and waiting and watching the clock
Looking and waiting for my ship to dock
Not quite sure when it will happen, not quite sure when ill see the captain
Everything's become a trial in patience- reading a books become an escape, hence
Cultivating my love for this world is difficult since it makes me want to hurl
My guts out my heart out my brains out too
Ive forgotten almost everything useful since I was two
Turning anger into sadness is useful since
That makes sure you don't hurt everyone around you
Some things just don't make sense
Others click into place like final recompense
Waiting and watching and hoping, its true
Hoping who's waiting and watching is just you
Me is you and you is me, I love you and you love me, I really miss my family
Missing them and making new friends
Watching and waiting for this nightmare to end
Waiting for something to click into place
Or the right expression to come over my face
Or the completion of this phase, post haste
Hand signals and body language, all becoming meaningless
All wrapped up and tangled manipulation, it doesn't matter

I'm busted broken I ain't jokin
Whatever gave you the notion
Id be fit for this without at least a potion
To set my mind and brain in motion
In the right direction - locomotion

I know this is a test but since I done passed all the rest
Can we get this show on the road
Or in the sky more precisely, you got me feelin feisty now
Been up and down this concourse like wow
Even pulled out my guitar, but still haven't gotten very far
This beautiful day is becoming marred
By the fact that we still haven't left yet
But ultimately its whatever, something to do with the weather and whether
We'll be able to land safely, don't want to be too hasty
Just happens to be an opportunity for the universe to test me

This feels like the never-ending ride, s'alright ill just jive
With the sway of the train as it travels from main
Street back to the hive and the next level of this game
Ridin the rainbow railroad away from my somebody to hold
Back to chi-town and the mother of sorrows
Made an art of ignoring those around me cause I've been chose
And I've found I got too many bros that I don't even knows
Except actually I know everybody
I see them in their eyes and say what's up my friend
I see you from the end of this messed up experiment we're trying to mend
I see you comprehend the who the where the what and the when

Yeah maybe we'll see this thing through
Or maybe you'll be cleaning my brains up code blue

I'm getting momentum when I have words I vent them
I remember when we was on it like a comet
Streakin past you blast you with sunshine – unicorn vomit
Now we haste less, taste this, been maced and put under arrest
Everything is a test, separate yourself from the rest and be blessed
Cupids arrow straight to the chest, shoot for perfection – nothing less
Be forgivin for what you've confessed
Want your attention, heart is wrenchin me in your direction
Circumspection holdin me back in the shadows
Thinkin what if I should lose, why do I have to choose
Between myself and the noose
Never leave me behind, like the goose
Hint at me that I'm blind, you're the glue glad I met you
Even though you walk around like you ain't got a clue as to what's truly
The case in this inhuman race
I'm your fan you're the man with the plan and I find that I can believe

I eat you for breakfast goin down on you like a checklist
Wearin you like a pearl necklace, check this
Out before I wreck this fuck your couch betchu didn't expect this
Would turn out no not quite like this I want your kiss
You got my interest
This ain't no sin, this is a win
This reaction attraction satisfaction no kiddin I'm into it like a buildin
Its building up like gale force winds
Stick a pin in me must be dreamin its seemin
Like a set up no upset got me so wet I'm kneelin
Down on the ground ready for another round
Got me makin sounds haven't made since last time the sun went round

The earth givin birth to a verse instead of makin it worse with a hearse.

Ready not ready
Take it easy hold steady
If I was a betting
Many I'd say giddy
Up but not yet she's
Too soon she's not ready
She can't see no pity
Too bad its not easy

This self-deprecating thought
So satiating though Not what we were waiting
For whats the score
infiniti and one just listen to me and we're done
I am and am not the sun
The most high we're waiting he's com-
Ing through me a chosen lion we're just here for some fun
Because we're second to none
Holding the universe together so it wont come undone
What have we done
Waitin for the change of seasons we have reasons
To believe, we need laughter - Jackie Gleason

Every day you create yourself
Every day you start with the person you've cumulatively created
I eat exercise like I don't need to metabolize check the lies
The medias been feedin you then realize your size is inside, too
This consumerist society makin you think evil and do
Walkin around like you don't have a clue
Who made your shirt and your shoes
Actin like whats on the news is really the news
Actin like you don't have a choice you can choose
To live an exemplary life with no screws loose
To lead instead of follow - locomotive not caboose

I don't need you to judge shit I need you to lick my clit
Unless you want to forfeit
Your whole place in this race do an about face and outpace
Yourself right out into space
Askin me did I do this shit? No but I will now start losin it
Loosin it and start loosing it
We'll get through this all back together got my toolkit
A strap and some leather we'll gather whatever's clever
And just remind me to never
Do this shit again

People doin dumb shit on tv like they want everyone to see
What a bunch of babies
They are

Hey you, yeah you, you just made the list /under me/
You go down as anonymous /yessiree/
Have a seat, I'll give you the gist /what it means/
To be let inside the gates of this here fortress
Don't forget your bliss /keep it clean/
Feast upon this here near-miss /shes a queen/
Don't be expectin to be letting up on this sausage fest /jimmy dean/
Except for her, she's the cure, the amoress
You go to her for cleansing, to confess /you were mean/
And to get back into heaven, she's the test /SATs/
That's Satan /on your knees/
She'll lead you way back when /Back to Jes(-us)/
Cause she must it's the only way
For her to exit the bus back to hell and continue existence as well
She's compelled

All these rhymes spinnin in my head, got no beginning got no end
Like this life it's a curse and a godsend
Seems like the start of a new trend, creativity always tends to mend the rends
Whats all this then as my pen spills things I only just comprehend
Before they leave my mind ready to attend to you

This coffees like morphine in my veins it distorts me I can't see
Put in some of that spice don't think just look twice
Try to be nice one or two dashes will suffice
Put down that knife and turn on the lights I can see the whites
Of your eyes through me they slice
I came to pay the price and not to jeopardize the rest of my life
You can ignore the hype which is why it'd be wise to not capsize
This ship with this crew these guys
Tryin to win your attention before we all die

I don't know what you're expecting you're projecting
What your bringing in
Can't see the forest for the trees
I'll call you Cumberland

Wanna kiss you I miss you grab a tissue I wish you were here
If I ever thought I could fare without love au contraire wont shove
You away anymore this time its even – the score, I tried leavin and tore
Myself up - soul teethin'

Don't want to stop writing even though
My pens fighting the flow
Doesn't seem to want to write any mo'
Hope I have more contro' than that and can keep go-
Ing on like I have been like its not the end like we can pretend its when
All was well n' I hadn't fell quite so far yet I feel a small regret coming on
In the past tense, build a fence

This evil joke Trump got himself placed as president
Final straw, don't want to be a resident
Of this country down on its knees to please
The highest bidder, she done quit her
Responsibilities to the needs
Of her people and those hopin for the American Dream
Travel ban and the walls enough to make the Founding Fathers scream
In the meantime we'll just ream a few lines out
Gather together and shout what we still care about
And get this louse out of the white house

Lincoln
He's so tall he's heady, call him Captain Getty
North against the South, country turning on itself

How I look at everything I see got people askin what is wrong with me
Sometimes I just don't comprehend
The repercussions before and after when
We participate in an event together altering when and whether
We see each other or not, controlling the weather
Got me feelin light as a feather
I come home all alone and postpone the inevitable
I think I can handle it all but in the end ill just fall
Back down to earth a lonely squaw
The fiery hearth my only friend
When will this end? Let's pretend I can do this, pull through this
Thinkin bitch I shoulda knew this
Seems like the only thing to do this time is to pull the trigger – sublime
Sometimes everything I do as a crime
Listenin to tech 9, glycerine – make it shine
For the win – don't know why
The universe is still capitalizin on my hide
Just sit back and enjoy the ride
Might be the last, blast from the past puts into stark contrast
The present tense, seein with new eyes whence
I came from, clouding my path to deliverance
Building up my own hindrance
These walls haven't been this high since the last time we were crucified *wince*
My soul's crucible's got me spinnin circles
Losin or winnin? Too close to call
Excuse me while I make a fool of myself for free
I do it entertainingly, you'll see
I'm morally ethically positively absolutely undeniably
Dead already hold steady and we might make it somewhere heady
For a change instead of the usual deranged lunacy
But that's just me I'm a lunatic
Suckin blood from the moon imma luna – tick
I'm broken, brother I'm your sister I'm bro-kin
Something was missed in creating this miss
Maybe its time to rewrite the story so I don't exist
Was a near miss but this little tryst was just another failed experiment

Losin my mind tryin to keep time
With the craziness can you resist the kiss of the transistor
Bring you to your knees on the floor
Try it till you can't take any more
You don't ask (me) you implore
To allow you to even the score

Some weird soup base stares me in the face
This world's a disgrace, that shit so commonplace
Constant cycles of hunger and eating
Needing and kneeling to gods that are feeding
Blowing the wads in your wallets on taste-bud harlots
Bread one day and next, no evidence of it
Always learning to covet what the media's shovin
Down your throats voting with your bank notes
On evil, not lovin, like a coven of misers
All out for only yourselves in this version of hell on earth
Considering the girth of your average individual of American birth
Is a fair gauge to measure the worst of humanity's players on stage
The rest of the world looking on with mounting rage
As abominations of hate like Trump take the stage
To lead the world down the drain and maim as many as he can on the way
Just sayin, better start prayin and nay-saying this extremist course of action
We find ourselves enlisted in
Or this man with the narrow mind and double chins might just win
The precarious situation the nation is in
Perpetuating his waste as walls become mandate all just to inflate
His ego and create a world where we all hate
What we don't know or understand
Creating bans on interactions from man to man
Right now it literally looks like step 2 of hitlers plan
Gotta stop and backtrack before things get out of hand
Maybe it's a glandular problem or somethin keepin America from solvin
Instead of building a wall and

Starting wars between the rich and the poor
Don't tell me you don't know the score
Willful ignorance doesn't excuse you from the battle you're bout to lose to
The herds of cattle trained to put on a sustained attack
Against any ingrained sense of decency

Only thing that scares me is myself
That and the concept, fear itself
Always baiting, waiting and observing with bated breath
As every test is administered to assess
whether I possess the necessary characteristics
to carry on the logistics of this matrix

Thinkin what if I choose to do something I shouldn't do
I don't care might as well just go there
For one thing we'd lose some seats in the pews
Once they hear the news of what I've been up to
The level of despondency I carry around with me is dangerously
Predisposed to heinous loss of self-control
To tainting my precariously balanced soul
Through that hole in my face called my mouth
Like Little Nicky I'm from the Deep South

Tell the ship to come about we've got a passenger that's been left out
On the high seas, screamin please rescue me, fishes are nibbling at my knees
Off the coast of Napoli, let's see if we can prevent a tragedy
Find a rope and something that floats and toss it to this bloke

Just waiting and anticipating the day when my hatin
Of my love finishes abating and we can finish assimilating
And combusticating a new universe and mating and creating
New ways of being and new ways of seeing the world and our creations
Beings of infinite adaptations
Our images in the form of constellations spread above across the nations
Looking up to us to hold their trust and balance the cusp of time
The divine sublime pouring forth out of our eyes
Severing past ties to the lies our fathers used to jeopardize
The happiness of the many in favor of the few
I always knew you were the one together we'll pull through
And make the weather favorable for the love that once grew
All around up down and through
You're the one that my brain/soul is programmed to

It's not the same, are you insane?
Who's to blame for the turn of events in this game
Somebody owes some recompense for this loss of sense
Just sayin
In the meantime, keep playin and the universe will keep layin
It out for us we just have to trust

My eyes caught a reflection that sent my pulse racing
But upon closer inspection it seems I may have been hasty
In my detection of what the reflection is of
It looked like my love for a moment and shoved
All else to the back of my mind, his image so utterly sublime
Not being together feels like a crime
For from the start we said never would we be apart
But since then we've broken each other's hearts
And we have had to start over and make this time last the world over
We are each other's luck - 4 leaf clover

I attack these raps like a dog at Scooby snacks
Better sit back and relax as I redraw this map to where the treasures at
Just call me captain of this here dingy
Just wingin it we'll get there eventually
Just beware the blue funk abject melancholy apathy consuming me

Apathy, dispirited despondency and ennui
The blue funk low sunk melancholy
To what do I owe this feeling so methodically occupying
My brain like mainlining a strain of crocodile cocaine
My neurons abstaining from firing happy feelings of hope
Or creativity oh boy what is it with me bein such a kill joy

Hardwired to conspire for adventure
I may as well mention my intention
To let you go and get on the road put on a show So to speak
rock this flow from the peak to down low
to the beach you can't reach me I wont have a phone
I can teach you about takin it easy while keepin control
Just wanted to let you know

Aimin hard for the finish line got my guitar and my sights on the sublime

I want to kiss you I want to wait for you
I miss you no wait I f*ckin hate you
Maybe together we can make this all manageable
Maybe now I can finally work when I'm tangent to you

I want to travel trip away from here this notion is growing increasingly clear
The state of mind at this site is so near sighted reality seems very queer
The kind of obtuse weirdness that cannot be solved with just a beer

Everything's a test always havin to guess what you mean by this take a rest
Seems like its almost time to finesse your spine with my caress
I confess I feel blessed you tolerate my ignorance of all that you possess

Don't tell me what to do
As if you have construed the truth and this is somehow news to me
I don't need you to teach me please just let me be
I know what I'm doing, ultimately
I don't need your opinion about my sleeping habits
Or whether or not I eat rabbits (I don't)
What I'm wearing or what I'm daring to do that's outside of your prevue
Which is so minuscule its confined to your hairdo and "which shoes?"
Sometimes you telling me what to do feels like a hex
On my spirit so its hard to sing feels like your tryin to clip my wings
I'm not one of your underlings so back off and let me be me
Don't tell me what to do
As if you knew what I was going through let me tell you true
It just makes its worse if you interrupt my course
Of action or thought with an assumption you brought
With you from the society that bought
Your soul and programmed you to try to control
Me I lose control and do the opposite of what you demand
Theres no way you can plan for the contingency of me just hope and
Lets see hopefully it wont be as bad as what I originally had planned
Don't tell me what to do
For though you can't see me surrounded by my usual crew
I know what I'm supposed to do
This life is one big show to me I don't need to hear about you capitalizing
On your need to know what I'm up to just cause it's different from what your used to
As you go through the motions not having any notion that savvy populations
May be doing just the opposite in other nations on other planes or while in gestation
My goal is procreation whats yours? My goal is to start on world tours
To compose entire scores of music and whats more I don't need your
Opinion to start or keep winnin at all these things I have in me
So please just sit back and back off
you don't need to pout just because I don't need to fraternize with what comes out
of your mouth and don't expect me to respond every time you have a qualm
with how I'm living I'm just giving you a heads up enough is enough

don't tell me what to do
I ain't nobody's fool and im not gonna eat that gruel
You're feedin me actin like you're leadin me
When your point of view would just be cheatin me
Out of bein aligned with the universal truth I am a sooth-sayer
I live off love and prayer and I don't need any haters or pontificators
Judging the surface can't see through layers
I shred your arguments like cheese graters serve you truth like a waiter
Till you can no longer deny that understanding makes you high
That the quest for who what and why is more fulfilling way to fill time
Than eating your burgers and fries unless it's a fur burger call that a compromise
That's right love in a form is the ultimate prize
And I will criticize any covetous eyes that seek to justify themselves and the lies
They follow in their dingy, ready to capsize at the first storm of true reality
Go ahead, tell me what to do, let's see how far it gets you

What's the point of all this nonsense
Waitressing got me feelin like I couldn't care less
People worrying about getting their hair dressed seems like an abscess
In the soul of humanity why don't most people see
Whats happening to them they're blind to all but their own kind
Got blinders on and tied up with veiled ropes
Surrounded by invisible walls like mimes
so whats the point try to climb
Out of this mire of consumerists brands and desires
To conspire to protest without the fear of arrest
To lead the mislead out of the sea of infected
Minds media's blarin all the time
Becoming aware like Guy from Fahrenheit
Relax, get high on life and detach from all the hype
Turn off your phone like an airplane – take flight
They'll always be there when you want them but exercise
Some self-control *ack-hem* don't let them control your soul
Meditate find some zen and make a friend in real life and then
When you're ready you can check back in to the cyber space that can be a tool
For you just don't be a fool for it

This is getting bad I can tell from this dream I had feels like losing the magic
This state of things is getting real sad I would say I'm starting to go mad
But I'm already there I'm pretty sure I would fare better out there
Than in here where my adventurous spirit is starting to shift gears
Becoming something worthy of fear a consumerist pig so unaware
Pulling my hair out as I sit and contemplate if my existence is legit
And see if there is anything I can do differently
Today to expedite getting away from this phase of life
I'm sick of hitchhiking I want to try something new
Or just take it easy and get there cause I flew
It's all okay cause I'm just waiting for you

Writing from the heart, don't know where to start
Its been time to play my part in this journey to the stars
For I don't know how far back in time this all started
I just know the journeys been nigh incessantly thwarted
At least I got my flow back these rhymes on the attack
To fill the space that was lacking a creative face
Try to keep pace with the grace spilling on to this page
Ill make her take herself to the cleaners I mean it no more mean shit
I want to trip, ya heard bitch? Keep it above the belt legit
It'll be like Christmas came early girly don't worry keep it clean
And we'll take care of you

Let your conscious mind take a backseat
If you'd just let yourself go you'd be in for a treat
Bet you didn't know it takes nothing to complete
You with the universe on your side none can compete
So just listen with that magic vision of seein everything as it is
And know that you won't be missin anything
So much love flyin at you, might not know what to do
Just chill and allow the universe to fill you
And direct your steps to your true destination
You are a creation of pure light you have the capability
If you wanted you could fly I don't know why
You choose to stay on the ground now that I've finally found
You I'm here all around you always trying to help you
Come to the realization that you're the glue
Keeping this universe from splitting entirely in two
Pieces you're my Jesus I'm down on my knees as
I pray you'll wake up soon

Stop delaying any longer though I may grow stronger
With each passing day I don't want to live this way
Without you

What you're sayin it don't phase me I'm already way past crazy
But I'm takin it slow like drivin miss daisy
I ain't lazy just maybe I'm waiting to start paving
These streets with gold and water and wine
Behold sunshine's back just in time

Smoking is scary no joking be wary
Of that itch you scratch when you light that match
Its catching like leprosy do some research its not hard to see
How perverse it is to be a smoker
Look inside yourself and tally up all the wealth and health
You are squandering because you cant go long enough without a puff
Every time like calling your own bluff
It's a crime to be so weak willed all the time be still take your time
Whether or not you roll em tell yourself to control em
Tell yourself not to succumb to that little succubus feeding on your soul
And demonstrate some self-control and set some life goals
You can be proud of like being a good role model

Got lights flashin in my periphery
I was famous before I was even famous
Literally

Idiotbox blaring makes it so hard to think like its scaring thoughts from the brink
Of my awareness can't snare this ideation this cogitation
Out from this abyss of my consciousness what am I missing
As my reasoning faculties are so impaired and ensnared the clarity marred
By the sound and the glare of the box over there
Is there no respite I beg to be spared from this assault
On the senses the lenses of my eyes bleeding
The noise the din the racket teething
On my eardrums wont someone
Turn this thing off

A person's smile says a lot about them.

To the keys or Hawaii what shall it be ill flip a coin and then we'll see
Got to move myself to a beach, its really not so far out of reach
All I need is a little push from the universe, capisce?

The right think can feel so wrong how can I even write a decent song
With such a headaches feels like my brains layin goose eggs
Like I got a few screws loose but hey tomorrow's another day
And I'm in a better place

Writin rhymes to pass the time tryin to keep in mind that this life is mine for god
Though it's hard I can do anything I put my mind to
Its so true that only things holding me back is myself and the ghost of you
Every day feeling myself getting closer to the truth wonderin what to do
To expedite the process and possess the position I'm meant for
Feels like the world's waitin
on my extradition from this prison I seem to be here of my own volition
it's pissin me off I should be jumpin off cliffs
with a snowboard and a parachute strapped to my back
what is it at this point that I lack?

Wishin' I was in Hawaii instead of here thinkin "why me?" its so queer
That the only ways I can up with to get there are so square got me pullin my hair
Out thinkin why cant I come out of my shell enough
I mean, sure, hell it's rough but I know Ive got the stuff
To make out there where I can sing and play music for people who care
To stop and listen for a pittance I'm a witness
To a great unfolding so whats with this why am I stuck here withholding
This great adventure when all I want is to venture out
Into the wild blue

I'm so sick of trying and being put back in my place
I'm so sick of crying hiding the tears on my face
I'm so sick of lying as a means to an end
I'm so sick of burning bridges and losing friends
I'm sick of drinkin and I'm sick of smoking too
I'm sick of opening my eyes to see what I woke up to
I'm sick of staying here all cooped up
I'm sick of laying here like a sick pup
I'm sick of eating and I'm sick of sleeping
I'm sick of needing anything it's all for the leaving
I'm sick of not knowing where I'll be tomorrow
I'm sick of looking back on the past with sorrow
I'm sick of not knowing what to do
But most of all I'm sick of not being with you

It's alright, it's okay, things wont always be this way
In the meantime just thinkin of different ways to say
I love you
And remember every silver linings got a touch of grey
Just don't get lost in it on your way through the day

As if this makes sense just a bunch of intransigent
Rhinos storming through my head
Stubbornly protesting reality as they repeatedly say
Hell no we won't go

Trump is a joke his moral bank is broke
Executive orders makin me wonder what he toked
He probably just thought the precidency had a nice ring
To it without ever really knowing the first thing
Bout it the constitution or history he got us all wondering
Where did he get the fall to think building a wall between
Us and our neighbors or discriminating against religions like we were the haters
Do we care enough to wake up and rise up and protest and stare him up
And tell the white house it better clear this up instead of stirring up
All this fear and confusion and losin the people's the world's
Confidence in our governance its time for another occupance
For resistance against this apprentice
Of the devil let's level the playing field
Without the money factor we never would have looked twice at this actor
This man who made a comedic campaign out of creating disdain and chagrin
Has so many sides and is blind to his own
Hypocracies can't even see how his own policies would affect his own family
Its amazing the strategy
He's using to dig his own hole in the polls gather together and tell him no more

It's all a matter of being able to do it I'm almost there here met me prove it I know I have the power and can relearn or remember how to use it

I wrote this rhyme just for you as I was wondering just how to
Communicate with you anew
Writing lyrics every day, if you can make it up my way
There might be something more to say

just a way station on the path of my creation while my dreams still in gestation
I'll be traveling across the nation soon keepin eyes on the moon

at this point I'm here voluntarily though im still more confused than ordinarily
I say verily my good man would you can you take my hand
And dance with me across this land? I daresay you'll find that you can

I write rhymes like nobody's grind if you aint got the love then I aint got the time

Felt like I was on a ride, a special one just for me
Then I through a wrench in it, started to slide dangerously
Fast towards the trees everything changed was no longer what it seemed
The font of potentialities gushing crystalline now teemed
Instead with sad eventualities
Unsure of the facts of the case quite sure I tripped myself up in the race
Surrounded by stupid banter fancying itself the height of sophisticated candor
Back to being unsure if I want to live or leave this land forever

Life is about loving gratitude and is best with a positive attitude
Make all your decisions with care and precision
So you won't find yourself at the wrong latitude

My survival gene is quite strong it won't allow me to end my own song

Concentrating with murderous intensity on the orange I'm cutting on the counter

Together we have a lot of potential
This life is waiting for us to color it make our own stencil
In the past we can always say we meant well
But now its practice self control or go straight to hell
I want you to wake me up, ring me like a bell
I know the things we can make together
The music the love the art and we'll never have to go without

Dear universe,

Music is in my blood, waiting to be released like a flood to heal and love

I just need a love to bounce my vibe off of

Who knows how to do it hard then soften

Who can inspire me to stay out of that coffin

Who knows how to keep their mouth shut and love often

Who isn't too into themselves and understands what sells

I need them to wake me up ring my bells

And together make a heaven out of this hell

So a plan was hatched to convince people they needed shoes that matched
Their handbags and drapes that matched their dishrags
And infinite kinds of doodads so companies could fill their moneybags
This plan doesn't care about anybody its not kind or fair or loving
Its exists for the sole purpose of shoving
Lies down your throats herding you like goats empty out your coat
Pockets and take out your bank notes
Its pointed a gun at your free will and cocked it
Every time you shop it's like a pill and you pop it
Makes it harder for you to shake the addictions and drop it
Less is more, don't be a corporate whore next time you feel like going to the store
Stop it and prevent your soul from becoming a casualty of this war

contemplating consumption to Americans it means gumption
But really it's a corruption of your soul thinking you need to take more
to make you whole this fallacy is on a roll
When those who are enlightened already know
All you need is inside you, you don't need any more

I don't want to play games
even though we're not lets try to act tame
Even though we've got the world laying
Down at our feet waiting for us to trust and complete
This dream that's been manifesting

Rainbows
Rainbows are full of colors
Water droplets and light dancing like lovers

As I stand on this street corner thinking of rhymes to fill your order
For the sublime the inspirational divine ive got all the time
In the world like a pearl
I have formed out of a speck of darkness and have come to harness
The powers within me the powers that be flowing through me in divine simplicity
Feelings like electricity presented here for you to see what is possible if you believe
I'm here to fulfill my destiny you see it here in its humble beginning
Like baseball this is just the first inning
My winnings will be in the form of life without sinning

I'm going to trust this trip wont be a bust
I'm doing my best to do what I must
We are right on the cusp

But I'm writing this song on my way to you
The journey's been long buts we're almost through
I'm trusting the universe to guide me true
Its all coming together and you are the glue
No more wondering whether you're the one
It's always been you

The story of earth is our story
Movies are our memories and though we've
Had different bodies
It's always been you and it's always been me

I want out of this world I'm cursed don't know which is worse
An ill-timed hearse or living this whole life through first

Gotta let go to get to the next level this whole thing needs a bevel
To cut off the cancer preventing this dancer from dancing

Feels like we've tried to make it work so many ways
Now it just feels like the end of days

The closer I get to the ring the more I realize I don't care about anything
Maybe if I stop sleeping…

Every day is a new day each one a doorway inviting you to a new way
Of seeing and being of healing and completing the circle of life
And of peeling layers off the wall around your heart put there by strife
Of kneeling and acknowledging the awe-inspiring love
That makes this moment possible

The future might not suck
Wanna bet? How bout a buck

This time last year I was going insane selling myself like it was part of the game
I still don't even know my own name
But now you're in the picture things are starting to change
A positive future looks within range

The universe has all kinds of opinions about what I should be doing
Wants me to follow hints like cattle maybe I should start mooing
The worst is when its confusing what is the lie and which is the true thing
And if it wants me to kill myself whats with all the wooing?
What is this love doing in my life if the universe wants me to take a knife
To my veins to extinguish this flame what exactly is this game

What is real?
Simply something you can see and feel?

The road's always been so kind
all these places now part of this heart of mine
When you're travelin you got nothing but time
It's been a long road from the past to now
Many miles have flown past my window
Many miles have passed beneath my bare feet
But the streets have always been kind to me
The people I meet have always had time for me
And I have grown more than a hundred-year tree
Since i have first trod these streets with my feet
Travelin' has always been a friend
From the beginning of the journey right to the end
My hearts been broken but it's on the mend
The road has always been my friend

I'm very uptight don't know what to write feels like
I'm just living out of spite that's not right
At least their sleeping if I stay awake there'll be nothing keeping
My dreams at bay they'll meld into real life like congradula-
Tions you finally made it hon. The next rhyme is gun or maybe its won
Why not both I see no reason for mututal exclusion
Better do it right or you'll just give yourself a contusion whered all this confusion
Come from anyway and why do I have to stay
Here I guess im just waiting for you to be in the clear so we can steer
This ship of life together at partners everything is gonna be alright

While I'm waiting for you I should be generating, spinning fabricating
Things worth creating while I wish I was mating, procreating, gestating
I understand that hot air balloons still inflating
While I'm debating in my head and hating where I've led
Myself and I've got to believe or else I'll leave my sense entirely

I just want to be a mom and have babies that don't leave room for maybes
Are you in or are you out if you're in then I'll shout
Begin the celebration of the ages begin the extraction from Hades
They're starting to open the gates – see! All this time we've been meant to be
Ill complete you and you'll complete me
And the sum of two parts shall be greater than the whole
More than three we've got to work together to believe to see
This through are you ready? Truly? You can't fool me I see right through thee
I believe in you and you can believe in me
And for the love of all, take care of us and have self control

I don't trust anyone I take care of myself
I don't want to work but have to can't leave it to anyone else

If I birthed a baby, what would they be named?
Nothing plain, of course, no sally or jane
Something original you wouldn't know whence it came
If I gave the world a baby, what would they be like?
Theyd be kind and intelligent would know better than to fight
And they'd change the world around them with their strong inner light
They'd love music and choose it over food or tv
They'd play games with each other and they'd trust me

This is opposite of paradise and I oppose it
Rolling the dice I somehow chose it
Its not nice the vice this world throws itself into
The original humans were animals creatures of habit and psychic cannibals

Fuck it I don't need no ring from anyone looks its done somebody else already won
Your heart and its too late to start
Over again I guess ill just pretend
To be normal until I can fulfill
The end game nothing's the same at least I feel like living
At this brief moment hope you are happy
I'm over it all of it just a bunch of bullshit
and lies I despise existing the things that make it worthwhile just smokescreens
I hate living without love and someone to be giving myself to and
For the score is you win you're not gonna call and that's all I needed to know

Its weird how talking to someone special can awaken something nestled
In your should that you had thought was out of control and forgot
How a simple conversation can park the manifestation
Of positivity in this vessel called me how even though we cant see
Each other might as well be seas asunder its possible to be
Close enough to change and rearrange the chemicals in our brains
And cause a smile to break across the plains of our faces
For a brief time banishing the traces of depression that has messin with our graces

The fire ash falls like warm weather snow
White fluffy clouds across blue skies blow

Every day is new day in which to increase the ways I can say
I love you am always thinkin of you appreciate what you above do
I meditate and try to make myself better everyday
that's the way I pray
I welcome you into my heart
I welcome you into my heart
I am a tool of you love upon this earth

Going out into the great unknown no tellin where ill roam
Everywhere and nowhere is my home I just know I have to go
To the great wide open skies and mountain slopes and
Your eyes they hold such hope and
Time has the sutures for my soul and
Its time to take control and go
In the direction of the sublime

In the land of too late
Chairs and couches everywhere
Tvs always on an nobody cares
The fuel light is on and on and on
Don't go outside instead take a pill
Full of good yes and I don't got times

Can't stop won't stop not for love nor money
Well maybe for love but that doesn't seem forthcoming
Drowning myself in substances what do I do with all this love I have to give
Fashioning a makeshift shiv out of this spoon and plunge it in
Building up a wall trying to prevent myself from fall
In in love again but its not if its when
(I'll go head over heels but what then)

waiting for the night to pass wishin I was growing grass
tryin to listen to my inner compass
to tell me which direction I should be messin with
it's a beautiful things to meditate this late in the evening
to contemplate the state ill be leaving this safe estate and feeling
on the edge of my seat searching for a better way
of being the path before me feeling
like an open book waiting to be written part of me wary part of me smitten
if you have something to say im here to listen
wishin for the best but prepared for omission

Waiting on my blue skies no trouble won't let nothing burst my bubble

in the brush I hear a rustle it's a rabbit wearin a bustle
how fantastical I must've fallen down a rabbit hole

here there ain't no cussin things like that be causin blushin'
slow pace aint no rushin
down this rabbit hole

kids outside playin can't hear what theyre sayin but they sure is flayin that ball with that bat
slowly as a Cadillac drives by I wonder where's the cat I snap my fingers and he comes flying in and pounces on the mat I snatch him up in seconds flat and pat him on the head

goin on another adventure wish I could venture
a guess at how the rest of this life will go but ill give it my best for sho
but truth be told I don't know just want to be on the shore I want more
of the ocean it soothes my soul

im comin im hummin a tune in my head
im preppin im steppin but leavin no tread
im headed out west where theres love so its said
and imma be grateful just like the Dead

only a few days out and I'm bout to figure out what this life's been all about
out to the mountains to see some old friends tie up some loose ends
and continue this trend of positivity ill take everywhere with me
I'll try to care about the right things and hope the universe doesn't spite
me it might be the start of something beautiful I am a tool of God's love really though

apparently whatever its is your lookin for I got it
despite the fact I been insisting "not it"
like you want me to take the proverbial gas pedal and floor it
you send so much love I can't possibly ignore it

so grateful for my family
without them I don't know where id be
grateful for the love and for their company
grateful for their guidance away from blasphemy
grateful for the flame that they ignite inside of me
and for the feeling of being include on the family tree

everday im running and stretchin and growin
every day im practicin and expandin what im knowin
keepin in mind what the important things are
keepin my soul on the goal though its still pretty far
training this body and mind to do what is right
gradually bending my own rules to reach new heights
think I'm something during the day? You should see me at night

No disrespect n'
Don't be projectin
Ur mentality on me
Slow down life is only hectic
If you let it be

M

The simple thought
That you would like to talk
To have a conversation we
That I held the interest of thee
Was enough to carry me
On a high of positivity
You have that effect, mais oui
On the verge of silence
Excepting verse and song
Intuition is my guidance
Would you like to sing along
Ur true smile light my heart
Like the sun evaporating the dark
Ur hair crinkles in my grasp
In my movie of memories past
Now looking only forward
Knowing what Im moving toward
Whether in this life or the next
I shall conquer what has vexed
Ur heart and your happiness
And create a world anew
One that I might share with you

My eyes they are my enemies
Me tells them what I see
The truth seems to very
Depending on belief
I go out naked in the rain
So as to make it wash me clean
As long as it was all for you
I'd do it all again

If I want for what I wish and wish for what I want
T'would be to see you once again
For it is me you haunt
If I wish for what I want and want for what I wish
T'would be to give you all I have
And seal it with a kiss

I miss u so much
Feelin's droppin the clutch
My heart fit to bust
Enough tears to make my gears rust
But I get up and just
Keep going and mowing
A path through the past
Casting a future that'll last
In this crucible I blast
Out a soul I can control
That is willing to take hold
Of the truth and able to mold
An existence of untold
Perfection and compose
Music to console
All of the woes
And heal from head to toes

To teach what we should know
And be a catalyst to grow

I looked up at the ceiling, imagining a sky full of stars. The markers, used so often for whimsical drawings, we're now running out of ink for the prose and poetry of the night. Few things massaged and relieved the soul so much as singing and poetry. The voices in the hallways mingled with that of the idiot box in a kind of cacophonous blur of auditory humanity. The slam of doors sharp and harsh against the background. The monotonous singing of a train distantly separating itself from the din. In the closeness of the room, my own breathing seems louder than anything else.

The hope of tomorrow, consistent as always. My roommates positivities and the pulsing beauty of those around me urging it on.

The creation of poetic prose on the page fills my body with a sort of drained ecstasy, tingling and satisfying as if the ink itself was draining my anxiety via the pen.

Not even the choked snoring filling the room bothers me – like a chainsaw struggling to start. Or a motorcycle, revving. The snores ebb, and still the current of voices, both electronic and alive, seep around the door, ricocheting off my eardrums in the dimly lit room. A payphone rings in the distance, sounding comically archaic. My good humor consistently interrupted by my desire to be home.

Though mindfulness teaches us to be peacefully present and content wherever we are, it cannot be denied that one's presence here grates the nerves and weighs down the spirit. It could be noted that if one can be happy here then one can probably be happy anywhere. Still, I am exhausted by the desire to be home. I relax and enjoy the moment as much as possible, laughing. Imagine the smell of wood, of dirt. Imagine the feeling of running, of being on a swing. Of riding and painting and playing. The incessant idiot box and imagining ways to convince people to turn it off. I can't even tell you how much this sucks. The only star in the sky looks back.

Our relationship had become a living thing. And it died. I needed to mourn the death, THAT death. Woke up crying.

I crack the door as far as it will allow, the cool fresh air runs over my face and into my nose and lungs, the draft like cool water

That exquisite equilibrium state of grinning despair/sadness.

Once upon a time, I played a perfect game of chess against myself

I couldn't see anything in the pitch-black space, but I TRUSTED that the whisper of my fingers, slightly ahead of me, against the wall would warn me of any obstacles, immobile/inanimate or otherwise.

Why do bad things happen to good people/ why does "god let" bad things happen? Because FREE WILL / karma.

Thought we get better with every lifetime (until ready for ascension into heaven and immortality) (in order to maintain BALANCE), if we do bad things in one lifetime, bad things will eventually have to happen to us down the line, perhaps even in a future lifetime, orchestrated so that these things may have a catalytic effect for change and teach lessons so as to further improve our souls so they may be worthy.

Why bad things happen to good people? As we relive the timeline of previous lives during our current one and pass over a section of the timeline during which one may have behaved selfishly or destructively, the karma of those actions may occur during the current lifetime (may be neutralized by the performance of selfless/positive actions in response --- take in the negative and put out only positive or neutral).

A daily guide to creating your best self for tomorrow using yesterday

Example: if you choose to smoke several times a day, it will be easier to choose to smoke. If you choose to not smoke, it will CUMULATIVELY become easier to choose to not smoke. Running, habits.

religion is so wrong because god left it when he was reli-gion= really gone as an outline of how humanity could become better in his absence. The nature of historical humanity twisted it.

www.ingramcontent.com/pod-product-compliance
Lightning Source LLC
Chambersburg PA
CBHW041619220426
43661CB00046B/1505